SPOTLIGHT ON THE CIVIL RIGHTS MOVEMENT™

FREEDOM RIDERS

LISA A. CRAYTON

Rosen YA™
New York

Published in 2018 by The Rosen Publishing Group, Inc.
29 East 21st Street, New York, NY 10010

First Edition

Library of Congress Cataloging-in-Publication Data

Names: Crayton, Lisa A., author.
Title: Freedom Riders / Lisa A. Crayton.
Description: New York: Rosen Publishing, 2018. | Series: Spotlight on the civil rights movement | Includes bibliographical references and index. | Audience: Grades 5–10.
Identifiers: LCCN 2017013901| ISBN 9781538380291 (library bound) | ISBN 9781538380260 (pbk.) | ISBN 9781538380277 (6 pack)
Subjects: LCSH: Civil rights workers—United States—History—20th century—Juvenile literature. | African Americans—Segregation—Southern States—History—20th century—Juvenile literature. | African Americans—Civil rights—Southern States—History—20th century—Juvenile literature. | Civil rights movements—Southern States—History—20th century—Juvenile literature. | Southern States—Race relations—History—20th century—Juvenile literature.
Classification: LCC E185.61 .C89 2018 | DDC 323.1196/073075—dc23
LC record available at https://lccn.loc.gov/2017013901

Manufactured in the United States of America

On the cover: The group of courageous men and women—black and white—who defied the practice of segregation through their Freedom Rides faced anger, hatred, violence, and jail time to stand up for their principles.

CONTENTS

DESTINATION FREEDOM

Thirteen passengers in Washington, DC, got ready for the trip of a lifetime. The eager group comprised men and women, black and white, and professionals and students. They were headed to New Orleans, Louisiana.

Boarding the buses for the two-week trip was easy. Refusing to obey racist Jim Crow laws while traveling was more difficult. On board, they would all sit side by side. They would resist in southern states when told to segregate themselves. At each stop, they would further defy segregation by ignoring posted signs marked "Colored Only" and "Whites Only" and venturing into facilities not designated for them. It was a bold, courageous plan.

At this midpoint in the civil rights movement in the United States, they put their lives on the line when they boarded that

Courageous Freedom Riders boarded buses and rode through the South to protest and end segregation.

bus in May 1961. Many made out wills before departing. Yet, their daring acts inspired others to do the same. Collectively, they changed interstate travel. Who were they? These audacious citizens were called the Freedom Riders.

ROAD WARRIORS

From its humble beginning of thirteen individuals, the group of Freedom Riders rose to more than four hundred people. Each helped the movement succeed. Some notable participants included John Lewis, Jim Zwerg, and Diane Nash. Then a college student, Lewis was on the first bus and rode out the entire campaign. Beaten and jailed multiple times, he did not turn back. His resolute commitment inspired others.

To whites who embraced Jim Crow laws, Zwerg was a traitor to his race. An iconic photo of him—lying in a hospital bed with a beaten, bloodied face—proved to the world just how badly segregationists wanted to maintain the status quo. Undefeated, Zwerg encouraged people to keep riding.

Concerned about Freedom Riders' inability to continue past Montgomery, Alabama, Nash urged students in Nashville, Tennessee, to step up for freedom. Her involvement is credited with sparking a participation revival.

John Lewis, now a congressman from Georgia, was an original Freedom Rider who provided important leadership throughout the successful nonviolent protest.

SIGNS OF THE TIME

Based on existing federal law in the 1960s, blacks had the right to travel across state lines and receive equal treatment as whites. But state laws allowed for unequal treatment. Dubbed Jim Crow laws and mainly enforced in the South, they covered racial interactions.

Back then, black people were referred to as being "colored." Visible posted signs directed everybody to "Colored Only" and "White Only" facilities and entrances. "White only" facilities were cleaner, nicer, and better maintained. Whites could walk through front doors of stores, restaurants, and other places. Blacks were required to use rear entrances and sometimes were denied access.

On public transportation, things were just as bad. For instance, blacks had to ride in the back of the bus. They had to give up their seats for whites if the front seats were full. They also encountered threats and violence, especially in the South. Freedom Riders changed that. They demanded—and won—equal and safe transportation and facilities for black passengers using local and interstate transportation.

Visible posted signs like this one directed everybody to "Colored Only" and "White Only" facilities and entrances.

OPENING DOORS

The Freedom Rides boldly tested states' enforcement of US Supreme Court decisions barring discrimination during travel between states. The Supreme Court is the United States' highest court. Its rulings apply to all states, which do not have a choice whether to obey.

One of the Supreme Court's 1946 cases was *Morgan v. Virginia*. The ruling banned segregated seating on buses. In 1960, in a case called *Boynton v. Virginia*, the court ruled segregation illegal in interstate travel. Its decision set a new standard prohibiting such discrimination.

After the court's ruling in *Brown v. Board of Education* in 1954, states could no longer rely on the 1896 *Plessy v. Ferguson* case. This ruling had permitted "separate but equal" treatment of blacks, but it was used as a basis for Jim Crow laws. Though states were supposed to stop segregating buses, they did not.

Bus companies permitted segregated seating by claiming they followed state laws. After the *Morgan* ruling, states were supposed to abandon those discriminatory practices. As the Freedom Rides proved, that did not happen.

This is the cover of sheet music for a collection of "Negro" melodies. The title uses the term "Jim Crow," referring to a caricature of a black man in a song and dance act in the nineteenth century.

ROAD LESS TRAVELED

A civil rights group called the Congress of Racial Equality (CORE) drove the success of the Freedom Rides by organizing the action and providing training to participants in nonviolent tactics. This training simulated the hostility, humiliation, and physical and verbal abuse riders would encounter. It paid off. Participants successfully endured the brutal situations without fighting back. CORE also made sure Freedom Riders had bail money and legal representation.

Testing public transit was not a new idea. In 1954, black bus passenger Rosa Parks refused to give up her seat to a white passenger in Montgomery, Alabama. Her resistance resulted in a yearlong bus boycott and a change in local public transportation. Before that, CORE had conducted its Journey of Reconciliation in 1947 by sending sixteen men—eight of them black and eight

This commemorative US postage stamp depicts Rosa Parks, famous for her contribution to the civil rights movement.

of them white—on an interstate bus journey to challenge Jim Crow laws. While considered successful, it did not have the same impact as the Freedom Rides.

READY TO ROLL

On May 4, 1961, an interracial team of thirteen volunteers split into two groups of seven blacks and six whites. Some boarded a Greyhound bus, while others took a Trailways bus. The first Freedom Ride had begun!

CORE's director James Farmer and participants John Lewis and Jim Zwerg were included in the team of seven men and six women. As planned, they boarded the bus and sat together in interracial pairs. At stops, they deliberately tried to use facilities marked for the opposite race.

They attracted attention, of course. Some passengers grumbled. But the ride was mostly peaceful until May 8. That day, Joseph Perkins, a black Freedom Rider, tried to get a shoe shine from a white stand in Charlotte, North Carolina. He was arrested and jailed for trespassing. After refusing to pay bail, he stayed in jail for two more days until a judge found him not guilty based on *Boynton v. Virginia*.

A famous civil rights activist, CORE director James Farmer organized and participated in the Freedom Rides.

SOUTHERN HOSPITALITY

On May 10, the riders pulled into the Greyhound station in Rock Hill, South Carolina. There, they found growing opposition. John Lewis and his white counterpart, Albert Bigelow, tried to use a waiting area reserved for whites. They were mobbed. A female rider was also hurt. The attack was short-lived thanks to police intervention.

From May 10 to 13, the riders reboarded, heading through Georgia. In Atlanta, they met and dined with the Reverend Dr. Martin Luther King Jr. However, the May 13 dinner fell short of their hopes. They wanted King to ride along, but he declined. His advice for them: turn back!

King warned of planned assaults by hostile Southerners, including the Ku Klux Klan (KKK). This white supremacist group

The Ku Klux Klan built a reputation as a violent, white supremacist group. Here, Klansmen are initiating new members into their organization.

was infamous for its violent crimes against blacks, including murder by lynching. Because of the anticipated violence, King predicted that they would never reach New Orleans. With his dire warning ringing in their ears, the riders headed further south.

MOTHER'S DAY MASSACRE

The next day, the Freedom Riders left for Alabama using Greyhound and Trailways buses. It was May 14, Mother's Day. Menacing racists met the Greyhound bus in Anniston, Alabama. They viciously attacked it and slashed its tires, preventing its departure. Suddenly, a firebomb hit the bus. Everybody escaped, but many suffered from smoke inhalation.

The unsuspecting Trailways team arrived at the horrific scene. Angry whites rushed on that bus, beating passengers. The driver took off with the attackers on board! The attacks were not over. Racists attacked the bus in Birmingham, too. This time, the violence went on for fifteen minutes. The police had promised to allow the mob's actions for that amount of time before intervening.

Photographs from the Anniston fire helped spark outrage. The incident was later called the Mother's Day Massacre. Drivers refused to take the team any further. Thus, the Freedom Riders took a plane to New Orleans on May 15. It seemed the cause had been defeated.

Dazed Freedom Riders sit near their firebombed bus in Anniston, Alabama.

COURAGE TO RIDE

News spread rapidly on radio, television, and newspapers about the Alabama assaults. It reached members of the Nashville Student Movement in Nashville, Tennessee. The group was affiliated with the Student Nonviolent Coordinating Committee, known as SNCC (pronounced "snick"), which had gained a reputation for its successful protests leading to the desegregation of local lunch counters and movie theaters. They, too, were trained in nonviolent, direct resistance.

Diane Nash, John Lewis, and Jim Zwerg were some of the leaders of SNCC's Central Committee. They and other members embraced the idea of resuming the Freedom Rides. They believed the cause could succeed. And they did not want violence to win over nonviolence.

Ten members of the Central Committee were chosen to ride. The team of three women and seven men boarded a bus on May 17 from Nashville headed to Birmingham, Alabama. Unsure of the outcome, some wrote their wills before departing.

Media coverage of attacks against Freedom Riders, including Jim Peck, who is shown here being beaten, spread rapidly and helped mobilize new volunteers.

JAILED IN BIRMINGHAM

The trip from Nashville to Birmingham totaled about two hundred miles (322 kilometers). Jim Zwerg, a white rider, and Paul Brooks, a black rider, sat together. Birmingham's law prohibited integrated seating. When the bus carrying the Nashville students reached the outskirts of Birmingham on May 17, the two were arrested for sitting together and were jailed.

Eugene "Bull" Connor was the commissioner of public safety. As the top police officer, he made sure the remaining Freedom Riders were rounded up and jailed. In jail, the Freedom Riders encouraged each other and communicated by singing freedom songs. Their upbeat singing infuriated the guards.

The rationale for jailing the protestors? It was a safety measure. The protective custody would keep them off the street and

These Freedom Riders from Tennessee were waiting for a bus to take them from Birmingham to Montgomery.

prevent Birmingham citizens from hurting them. In reality, it was a scare tactic. Connor hoped the Freedom Riders would be persuaded to stay out of the city once released.

FREED!

On May 18, most of the team was released from jail. Commissioner Bull Connor had them escorted out of Birmingham late in the evening. The students were left without help or transportation. Meanwhile, Zwerg and Brooks stayed in jail a day longer. On May 19, they had to appear before a judge for the charges against them. Once the judge cleared them of the charges, they were released from jail and warned to get out of Birmingham.

Commission Connor had hoped the jail time would make the Freedom Riders wary about being in such a racially charged city. The Freedom Riders called for help. Rather than running away like Connor wanted them to, they headed back to Birming-

Birmingham was an important target city in the Freedom Riders' campaign because of its particularly oppressive Jim Crow laws.

ham. They met up with Zwerg and Brooks. Although they feared violence and did not want to go to jail, they were committed to their cause. If they had their way, integrated interstate transportation would soon be a reality.

MOBBED IN MONTGOMERY

Getting a bus out of Birmingham initially proved impossible. Drivers refused to carry the Freedom Riders because the KKK thronged the terminal. Finally, after the US government stepped in, they were able to board a Greyhound bus. It pulled out on May 20 with the Alabama State Highway Patrol flanking it. A helicopter hovered above.

Things changed when the bus reached Montgomery. The highway patrol left, and the Freedom Riders stepped off the bus. Suddenly, members of the KKK appeared and rushed at them. Quickly and viciously, they attacked the Freedom Riders, reporters, and others.

More Klansmen joined the melee. Among other Freedom Riders, Jim Zwerg was beaten unconscious, and John Lewis was also severely injured. The photo of Zwerg lying in his hospital bed helped fuel nationwide outrage. It also inspired numerous individuals to flock to Montgomery. The movement was energized.

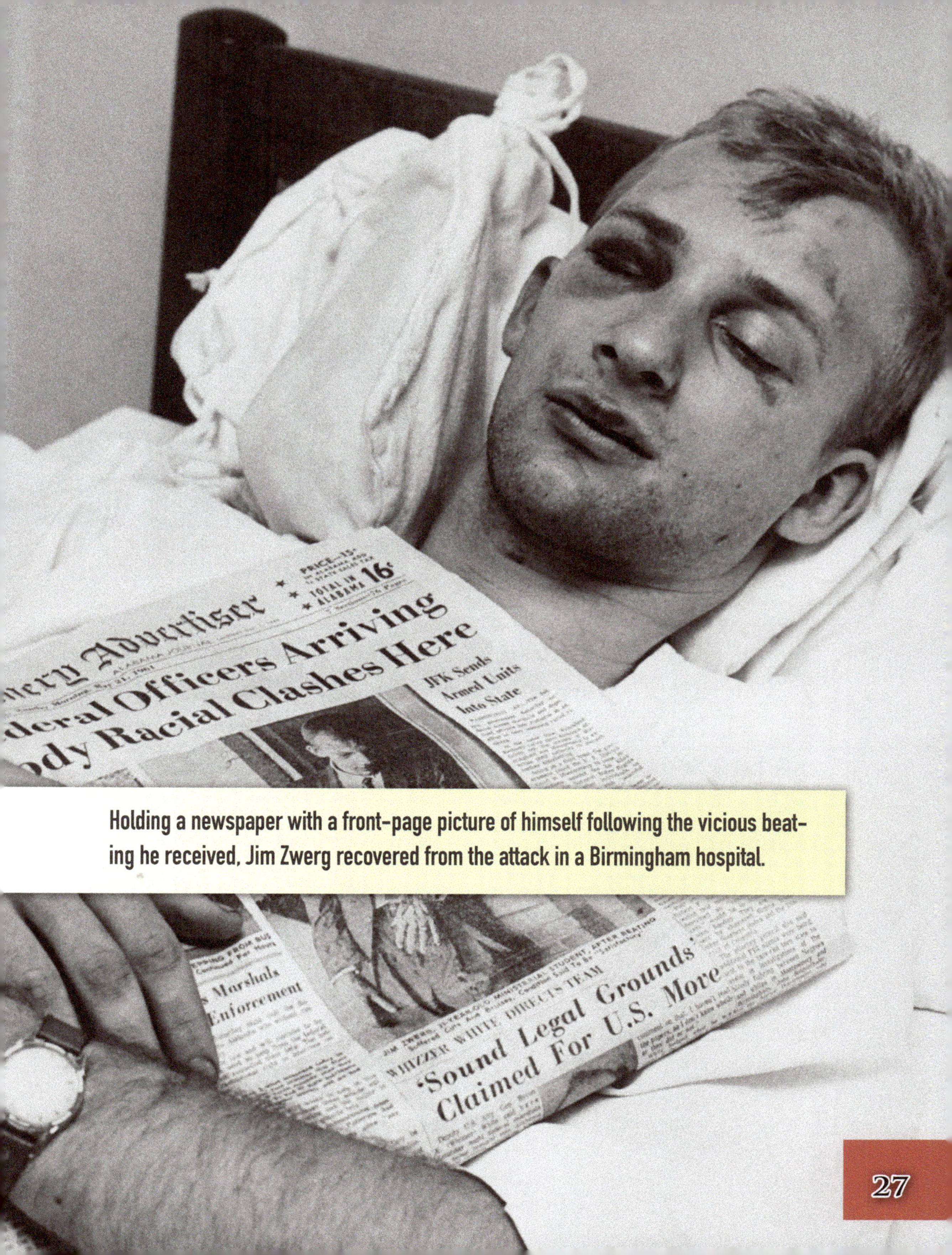

Holding a newspaper with a front-page picture of himself following the vicious beating he received, Jim Zwerg recovered from the attack in a Birmingham hospital.

MOVING TARGETS

First Baptist Church in Montgomery buzzed with energy on May 21, when its pastor, Reverend Ralph Abernathy, was joined by Reverend Martin Luther King Jr., Reverend Fred Shuttlesworth, James Farmer, and other civil rights leaders. In addition, more than a thousand others showed up to support and encourage the student activists.

The atmosphere changed as thousands of KKK members surrounded the church. The tense situation defused after state and federal law enforcement arrived.

On May 24, the Freedom Riders were back on two buses, this time headed to Jackson, Mississippi, and escorted by the Alabama National Guard. In Mississippi, they were

The National Guard protected the Freedom Riders and their bus, in order to prevent further violence.

immediately arrested. Many of the Freedom Riders refused to pay fines and were put in jail. But John Lewis and others were eventually transferred to Parchman, a state prison known for its cruel conditions and treatment of prisoners.

FACE OF RESISTANCE

Severe injuries sidelined Jim Zwerg. He spent his first two days in the hospital unconscious. He remained in the hospital for several more days after regaining consciousness. Then he left the city and flew home on May 25. It would take months for some of his injuries to heal, while pain from others never totally disappeared.

Meanwhile, many of his fellow riders went to jail. Stories about their valiant efforts continued appearing in the news. Pressure mounted for southern states to comply with interstate transportation laws. Meanwhile, the United States' reputation abroad was being affected. America was supposed to be a land of liberty, but if that was so then why were its black citizens being treated so poorly?

Attorney General Robert Kennedy sent in federal marshals to protect Freedom Riders and asked for a ruling to ban segregation in interstate travel.

Then, on May 29, US attorney general Robert Kennedy asked the Interstate Commerce Commission (ICC) to develop rules banning segregation in interstate travel. That request signaled a major victory for the Freedom Riders and the nonviolent resistance movement.

DRIVING CHANGE

Attorney General Robert Kennedy's request turned the wheel of change. Black passengers were getting closer to enjoying safe, hassle-free travel, especially in the South. However, the ICC took months before issuing its ruling. In the meantime, multiple Freedom Rides took place throughout the summer as waves of people were inspired by the Nashville students. These rides were sponsored by CORE and other organizations. They still exclusively focused on nonviolent resistance.

The itineraries varied. Departure cites included Washington, DC; Newark, New Jersey; New Orleans, Louisiana; Los Angeles, California, and St. Louis, Missouri. Final destinations also varied. They included St. Petersburg, Florida; Tallahassee, Florida; Little Rock, Arkansas; and New Orleans, Louisiana.

Freedom Riders included people of different races, genders, ages, and occupations.

Other destination cities were in Texas, Mississippi, and North Carolina. By the time the ICC made its rulings, more than four hundred people had participated in this successful nonviolent resistance.

SUCCESS

The wait was over. On September 22, the ICC issued its ruling, and it was a resounding victory for the Freedom Riders. Companies and states had to integrate their facilities by November 1. The ruling prohibited the segregation of passengers on board as well. Signs had to be posted notifying passengers of the change.

The ruling paved the way to fair and just treatment of blacks. No longer would they have to endure humiliating treatment from drivers and passengers. No longer could they be denied access to facilities. Gone were the “White Only” and “Colored Only” signs. Now, blacks could drink from any

The Freedom Riders whipped Jim Crow and eliminated segregated transportation, like these taxi cabs.

water fountain, eat at any restaurant, and sit on any seat on a bus. The Freedom Riders had accomplished the seemingly impossible. They had whipped Jim Crow!

ON THE ROAD AGAIN

November 1 arrived. The ICC regulations went into effect as ordered. Finally, blacks and whites were supposed to be treated as equals across the nation. But did that really happen? CORE was determined to find out. It launched new compliance tests of interstate travel. New Freedom Riders volunteered. They used the same nonviolent tactics that the team had used earlier in the year.

New trips from the North to the Deep South followed the same guidelines of the rides that had taken place earlier in the year. The results were encouraging. There was a difference. The Freedom Riders did not encounter violent mobs. Gone were the racist signs. And teams were allowed to sit in pre-

The Greyhound bus station that was the site of a horrific attack against Freedom Riders now houses a museum commemorating the rides and riders.

ferred seats and use desired facilities. Pleased with the results, CORE called the tests a success. Additional Freedom Riders were not needed. CORE could focus on other aspects of advancing civil rights.

LASTING LEGACY

Thanks to the internet, it is easier than ever to purchase bus or train tickets. Thanks to the Freedom Riders, black passengers traveling into the South do so easily. The civil rights movement continued to make great gains after the Freedom Rides ceased. Three years later, the Civil Rights Act of 1964 was passed. It banned discrimination based on race, color, sex, national origin, and religion.

In 1965, a goal of the civil rights movement became securing blacks' voting rights. The movement's leaders understood that if blacks had unrestricted access to the power of the ballot box, they would have more power to impact their communities and nation. That summer was known as Freedom Summer because of its emphasis on voting registration and sponsored education drives.

Thanks in part to those efforts, the 1965 Voting Rights Act was passed. Perhaps each of these accomplishments had such a lasting impact that the United States was ready—and able—to elect its first black president, Barack Obama, in 2008 and again in 2012.

Barack Obama made history when he was elected the forty-fourth president of the United States in 2008.

ALL ABOARD!

It has been more than fifty-five years since the Freedom Rides. The participants' accomplishments have been remembered in various ways. Early on, in 1961, the Nashville students received a Freedom Award. Since then, there have been other awards and honors.

Commemorative programs celebrate significant milestones. In 2001, a commemorative ride celebrated the fortieth anniversary of the original Freedom Rides. Ten years later, the Freedom Museum opened in the Montgomery Greyhound station where the Freedom Riders were attacked. Before leaving office in January 2017, President Obama issued a proclamation creating a Freedom Riders National Monument in Anniston, Alabama.

Original Freedom Riders take a ride to commemorate the fiftieth anniversary of the Freedom Rides.

No one could have predicted the phenomenal impact of the Freedom Rides. The story of the courageous individuals who boarded the first bus—and every one that left after that—lives on today.

GLOSSARY

audacious A person or action that is daring, bold, or courageous.

campaign Any series of activities focused on a specific purpose or outcome.

civil rights Rights given to all citizens that make sure they are treated the same and enjoy the same legal protections.

civil rights movement A fourteen-year period of sustained protests and activities designed to end segregation in the United States.

defuse To make less tense.

infamous Something or someone with a bad or evil reputation; notorious.

Jim Crow laws Laws enforced by states, mostly in the South, from the late 1890s until the early 1960s, to discriminate against blacks and segregate them from whites.

lunch counters Eating area in stores where people could sit to order and eat cooked food.

lynching A murder committed by a mob of people, usually by hanging the victim from a tree or other object.

melee A clash or confrontation.

National Guard A unit of the armed forces.

resolute Unyielding or determined.

segregate To separate things or people based on specific criteria, often used in terms of separating people based on race.

segregationist Generally used to refer to anyone who believes the separation of races is needed because one race is superior and deserving of special or better treatment, and vice versa.

status quo The present circumstance or situation; how things are currently.

will A legal document defining a person's last wishes upon his or her death.

Birmingham Civil Rights Institute
520 Sixteenth Street North
Birmingham, AL 35203
(866) 328-9696
Website: http://www.bcri.org
Facebook: @BCRI.ORG
Twitter: @bhamcivilrights
Instagram: @bhamcivilrights
The institute is committed to telling the story of the civil rights struggle such as the developments in Birmingham.

CBC Digital Archives website
Box 500, Station A
Toronto, ON M5W 1E6
Canada
(866) 306-4636
Website: http://www.cbc.ca/archives
Facebook: @CBC-Digital-Archives
Twitter: @cbc_archives
This archive houses videos of Canadian news programs, including ones about US Jim Crow laws and the Freedom Rides.

Congress of Racial Equality (CORE)
PO Box 264
New York, NY 10276
(212) 598-4000
Website: http://www.core-online.org
Facebook: @CORE-Congress-of-Racial-Equality-169681389720547
CORE provides numerous resources about its history, including audio histories, photo galleries, and information about the Freedom Rides.

Freedom Rides Museum
210 South Court Street
Montgomery, AL 36104
(334) 414-8647
Website: http://ahc.alabama.gov/properties/freedomrides/freedomrides.aspx
Facebook: @AlabamaHistoricalCommission
Twitter: @AlaHisCom
The museum is located at the site of the Greyhound bus station where Freedom Riders were beaten on May 20, 1961.

National Civil Rights Museum at the Lorraine Motel
450 Mulberry Street
Memphis, TN 38103
(901) 521-9699
Website: https://www.civilrightsmuseum.org
Facebook: @NCRMuseum
Twitter: @NCRMuseum
Instagram: @NCRMuseum
The museum features exhibits on centuries of African American history and is housed in the former hotel where Dr. Martin Luther King Jr. was assassinated.

Websites

Because of the changing nature of internet links, Rosen Publishing has developed an online list of websites related to the subject of this book. This site is updated regularly. Please use this link to access this list:

http://www.rosenlinks.com/SCRM/Freedom

FOR FURTHER READING

Aretha, David. *The Story of the Civil Rights Freedom Rides in Photographs*. New York, NY: Enslow Publishers, 2014.

Arsenault, Raymond. *Freedom Riders: 1961 and the Struggle for Racial Justice*. New York, NY: Oxford University Press, 2006.

Asim, Jabari. *Preaching to the Chickens: The Story of Young John Lewis*. New York, NY: Nancy Paulsen Books, 2016.

Bausum, Ann. *Freedom Riders: John Lewis and Jim Zwerg on the Front Lines of the Civil Rights Movement*. Washington, DC: National Geographic Society, 2006.

Lewis, John, and Andrew Aydin. *March: Book Two*. Marietta, GA: Top Shelf Productions, 2015.

Mahoney, Emily. *American Civil Rights Movement*. New York, NY: Rosen Publishing, 2017.

Mulholland, Loki. *She Stood for Freedom: The Untold Story of a Civil Rights Hero, Joan Trumpauer Mulholland*. Salt Lake City, UT: Shadow Mountain Publishing, 2016.

Sharp, Anne Wallace. *The Freedom Rides*. Farmington Hills, MI: Lucent Books, 2012.

Tisdale, Rachel. *The Freedom Riders*. New York, NY: Rosen Publishing, 2014.

BIBLIOGRAPHY

Aretha, David. *The Story of the Civil Rights Freedom Rides in Photographs*. New York, NY: Enslow Publishers, 2014.

Arsenault, Raymond. *Freedom Riders: 1961 and the Struggle for Racial Justice*. New York, NY: Oxford University Press, 2006.

Asim, Jabari. *Preaching to the Chickens: The Story of Young John Lewis*. New York, NY: Nancy Paulsen Books, 2016.

Bausum, Ann. *Freedom Riders: John Lewis and Jim Zwerg on the Front Lines of the Civil Rights Movement*. Washington, DC: National Geographic Society, 2006.

Bausum, Ann. "James Zwerg Recalls His Freedom Ride." *Beloit Magazine,* Winter–Spring 1989. https://www.beloit.edu/archives/documents/archival_documents/james_zwerg_freedom_ride.

Hasday, Judy L. *The Civil Rights Acts of 1964: An End to Racial Segregation*. New York, NY: Chelsea House, 2007.

Jackson, Tyra. "New Civil Rights Trail Debuts This Week in Anniston." *Anniston Star.* June 21, 2016. https://www.annistonstar.com/news/anniston/new-civil-rights-trail-debuts-this-week-in-anniston/article_beaa1b5e-3811-11e6-b32d-bb546db0c59e.html.

Levine, Ellen. *Freedom's Children*. New York, NY: Penguin Group, 2000.

Nelson, Stanley. *Freedom Riders. American Experience,* May 16, 2011. http://www.pbs.org/wgbh/americanexperience/films/freedomriders.

NPR Staff. "*Freedom Riders Reflect on 50th Anniversary.*" NPR, May 4, 2011. http://www.npr.org/2011/05/04/135985034/freedom-riders-reflect-on-50th-anniversary.

Schwartz, Heather E. *Freedom Riders. A Primary Source Exploration of the Struggle for Racial Justice*. North Mankato, MN: Capstone Press, 2015.

Ushan, Michael V. *Landmarks in African American History.* Farmington Hills, MI: Lucent Books, 2013.

ABOUT THE AUTHOR

Lisa A. Crayton is a former corporate publications editor and writer. Today, she is an award-winning writer and editor and has written for numerous religious and general publications. As a children's book author, she has written several books for Enslow Publishing. The events of the civil rights movement are an ongoing subject of interest to her.

PHOTO CREDITS

Cover, pp. 1, 5, 19, 27, 31 Bettmann/Getty Images; pp. 3, 42, 43, 44, 45, 46, 47 Onur Ersin/Shutterstock.com; pp. 4, 6, 8, 10, 12, 14, 16, 18, 20, 22, 24, 26, 28, 30, 32, 34, 36, 38, 40 Sergey Kamshylin /Shutterstock.com; pp. 7, 15, 35, 37 Library of Congress Prints and Photographs Division; pp. 9, 11, 17 Everett Historical/Shutterstock .com; p. 13 neftali/Shutterstock.com; p. 21 Underwood Archives /Archive Photos/Getty Images; p. 23 © AP Images; p. 25 Donald Uhrbrock/The LIFE Images Collection/Getty Images; pp. 29, 33 Paul Schutzer/The LIFE Picture Collection/Getty Images; p. 39 Evan El-Amin/Shutterstock.com; p. 41 The Washington Post/Getty Images.

Design: Nelson Sá; Editor and Photo Researcher: Xina M. Uhl